LEGENDS

35
GREAT
PLAYERS
— OF —
WIGAN RLFC

at heart ♡ publications

Observer WIGAN The voice of Wigan for 155 years

Acknowledgements

Thanks chiefly to John Riding for his encyclopedic knowledge and assistance in selecting photographs. Photographers Gary Brunskill, Nick Fairhurst and Frank Orrell were also a great asset, and Paula Gaster and Alison Hughes gathered and organised subscriptions. Thanks to the *Wigan Observer* readers who voted for their legends to represent the '80s, '90s and modern era, those experts who gave their opinions and invaluable insights of the legends from the other decades, and to those fans who subscribed for this book in advance.

First published in 2008 by
At Heart Ltd
32 Stamford Street
Altrincham
Cheshire
WA14 1EY

in conjunction with
Wigan Observer
Martland Mill Lane
Wigan
WN5 0LX

ISBN: 978-1-84547-190-3

Printed and bound by Ashford Colour Press, Gosport

CONTENTS

ABOUT THE AUTHOR

Phil Wilkinson was born and raised in Wigan, and still lives in the area with his wife Claire and two sons, Luke and Samuel.

He has been following Wigan since the day he was first perched on top of a crush barrier on the terraces at Central Park as a child in the mid-80s. He never managed to emulate his heroes on the pitch, prompting him to choose writing about rugby league instead.

He joined the *Wigan Observer* as a news journalist in 1999 and became sports editor two years later. Since then, he has overseen the sports coverage of a Challenge Cup triumph, one flirt with relegation and two Grand Finals.

This is his second book: *Season of Dreams* chronicled Wigan Athletic's first season in the Premier League.

INTRODUCTION

The word 'legend' is often overused in sport, but for many of Wigan RLFC's former heroes, the description seems almost limiting.

No club can boast as many of rugby league's greatest names as Wigan and now, to mark a century since the club's first Championship victory, 35 of their biggest names have been immortalised in this book.

Legends is a nostalgic celebration of some of Wigan's biggest names, a reflection on their wonderful talents and an illustration of their glorious conquests.

And that has been brought to life by some brilliant and often breathtaking photographs from the *Wigan Observer*'s archives.

Since their first championship triumph in 1908/09, scores of players have cast their legacies at Central Park and – more recently – the JJB Stadium, which made selecting the legends a painstaking task.

The *Wigan Observer* invited readers to select their greatest legends from the 1980s through to the present day and the response was overwhelming, with hundreds casting their votes for their favourite players.

A panel of expert judges comprised of lifetime enthusiasts, former players and coaches selected the greats from the pre-1950s to the 1970s. They all requested – and were granted – anonymity, but their input and insights proved invaluable in selecting Wigan's greatest names from the past century.

Some of the legends' careers transcended two decades. In those instances, judgement calls were made based not just on their career longevity, but on which decade their influence was felt the greatest. Andy Farrell, for example, graced the 1990s but captained Wigan to Challenge Cup glory in 2002 and won both the Man of Steel and prestigious Golden Boot as the greatest player in the world two years later. He has proudly been placed with the modern masters.

Inevitably for a club that has been graced by so many superb individuals, there are scores who have not made these pages. Apologies to those fans who marvelled at the wizardry and majesty of Billy Blan, Cec Mountford, Tommy Bradshaw and – more recently – Joe Lydon, Steve Hampson, Henderson Gill and Andy Platt.

This book would have become an opus if it attempted to include every great name from Wigan's history. Instead, it salutes 35 of the club's greatest names – from Ashurst to Ashton, Boston to Barrett, Egan to Edwards, Fairbairn to Farrell.

Phil Wilkinson,
Sports Editor, *Wigan Observer*

Jim SULLIVAN

Jim Sullivan, Wigan's finest.

Statistics don't always do justice to great players; in Jim Sullivan's case, they do a pretty good job.

In a playing career that spanned a quarter of a century, he made a staggering 774 appearances for Wigan and amassed a ground-breaking 2,317 goals; figures that have remained unrivalled.

Little wonder that experts widely consider Sullivan to be Wigan's greatest ever player. An immense athlete, the Cardiff-born full-back had already appeared for the Barbarians rugby union side and represented Wales at baseball before he started his Wigan career aged 17, on a reported 12-year contract.

His proficiency as a marksman helped Wigan to championship honours in 1921–22, 1925–26 and 1933–34 and Sullivan twice won the Challenge Cup with the Central Park outfit, in 1924 and 1929. It was during that tournament that he set a goal-scoring record that still stands, booting 22 goals in February 1925 against amateurs Flimby and Fothergill. Contemporary reports also salute Sullivan as a master tactician and a strong-tackling player.

Sullivan also played for Wales, England and 'Other Nationalities', and on his Test debut for Great Britain – against Australia at Sydney – he kicked a 65-yard penalty. He went on three tours (he rejected a fourth for personal reasons) and made 25 appearances for Great Britain, 15 of them as captain.

After retiring as a player at the age of 42 in 1946, he continued to serve as coach for a further six years before enjoying further success at St Helens. He returned briefly as coach in the early '60s, and was inducted into the rugby league Hall of Fame in 1988, 11 years after his death.

1921-1946

Jim Sullivan with the Challenge Cup trophy.

Sullivan scored more points for Wigan than any other player.

Ken GEE

Gee scored an impressive 508 goals during his career.

Unmissable in his distinctive skull-cap, Ken Gee was the cornerstone of the Wigan team in the post-war era.

A powerfully built man with deceptive pace, he signed from Highfield Juniors and went on to make a staggering 559 appearances for Wigan – second only to Jim Sullivan. Though Gee's career overlapped Joe Egan, the two were inextricably linked. They twice toured together with Great Britain in 1946 and 1950, and they played 327 games together for Wigan.

Gee was a competent goal-kicker from being a boy, but only took on that duty for Wigan towards the end of his career, finishing with a total of 508 goals.

He was a Wembley winner in 1948 and 1951, and shared in three Championship Final wins but like Egan, missed another two due to tour commitments.

He also won Lancashire Cup winners' medals an incredible seven times before retiring at the age of 37. His longevity and legacy was honoured with the creation of the Ken Gee Cup, a tournament that amateur clubs in Wigan compete in annually. Gee died in 1989.

1934 - 1954

Ken Gee wore a distinctive headguard.

Ken Gee's name will forever be linked with Joe Egan.

St Patrick's amateur club has been a nursery for rugby league greats over the years, and Joe Egan was one of their finest graduates; a point emphasised by a mural of him on their clubhouse wall.

Egan introduced a new style of play for hookers. Until he rose to stardom, the hooker's main function was to win scrum possession, but Egan became a huge influence on Wigan's attack in open play.

Without abandoning his traditional hooking duties, the former full-back became a proficient and influential play-maker – a style of play others later emulated.

He won his first trophy with Wigan in his third game and in a career that spanned more than 12 years he won 13 trophies, including four Championships.

Egan was made captain during the Second World War and had the unique honour of becoming the first player ever to receive the Challenge Cup from royalty when King George VI presented him with the silverware after the 1948 final triumph over Bradford Northern – Wigan's first Wembley victory since 1929.

He won the first of his 14 caps on the 'Indomitables' British Lions tour (named after the aircraft carrier they travelled on) that toured Australia in 1946 – their journey included a five-day train ride from Perth to Sydney.

Despite being 31, Leigh paid a rugby league record £5,000 for Egan in 1950. He returned to Wigan as coach, leading the club to Championship (1960) and Challenge Cup (1958 and 1959) glory.

Joe Egan meets King George VI at Wembley before
the 1948 Final, Wigan beat Bradford Northern 8-3
in front of 91,465 fans.

Joe Egan in full flow during the 1950 Australia tour. Egan made 362 appearances for Wigan between 1938 and 1949. He later captained the side and then coached the team between 1956 and 1961.

Martin Ryan was not only one of the greatest in his position, he also redefined it, and the modern full-back's counter-attacking style can be traced back to this great pioneer.

Until he emerged from the St Joseph's School Old Boys team into the Wigan side, the position required a player to catch, kick and occasionally tackle.

Ryan revolutionised that by applying the skills he had honed as an elusive centre into his new role at full-back when he succeeded the giant Jim Sullivan.

His approach reaped instant rewards during the post-war era, and he was a superstar in a side that won five Championships between 1944 and 1952. His link with half-backs Tommy Bradshaw and Cec Mountford was a potent attacking weapon, but he never neglected his traditional duties: a fabulous try-saving tackle on Trevor Foster helped Wigan beat Bradford 8-3 in the 1948 Challenge Cup Final.

His club career brought him 67 tries, as well as 63 goals in his occasional role as a place-kicker, but it was for the way that his skills in attack and defence blended with the team as a whole that Ryan is remembered as one of the club's greatest full-backs. He also made his mark for Great Britain, despite an unfortunate first tour to Australia in 1946, when he only played four games because of injury.

Ryan toured for a second time in 1950, winning the last of his four caps in a 6-4 victory over Australia in the mud at Sydney. He had played all three of his Ashes Tests and underlined his stature as one of the greats by holding his own against his opposite number – Clive Churchill, one of Australia's finest ever players.

Ryan served Wigan as a director after retiring. He died in 2003.

Ryan was a pioneer of the full-back role.

Ernie Ashcroft was a prince of centres.

A classic three-quarter, he made 530 appearances for his hometown club Wigan by the time his 16-year career came to an end, placing him third on Wigan's all-time appearance list behind Jim Sullivan and Ken Gee.

His 241 tries puts him sixth on the club's all-time try-scoring list.

Ashcroft attacked with flair and poise, and possessed the rare ability of always appearing to have time on his hands.

He broke into the Wigan side during the Second World War at the age of 17 and in the post-war era – and after switching from the wing to the centre – helped the club acquire a glittering array of silverware.

He claimed five Championships between 1944 and 1952, won the Challenge Cup in 1948 and also enjoyed Lancashire Cup and Lancashire League Championship glory.

Ashcroft played 11 times each for England and Great Britain before moving to Huddersfield as player-coach. After succeeding another Wigan great, Cec Mountford, as coach of Warrington he made a cameo comeback.

During Blackpool's first game at Wigan,
representatives brought captain Ernie Ashcroft a stick
of rock to mark the occasion.

Ernie Ashcroft scored 241 tries for Wigan.

1950s

Brian McTIGUE

He became Wigan's greatest ever prop, but it was only by chance that Brian McTigue even played rugby league.

Born and raised in the town, he never played the sport as a schoolboy, and instead cut out a name for himself as a promising boxer that reportedly included a professional fight at cruiserweight at the age of just 15. He was so highly-rated in boxing that former world champion Joey Maxim invited him to the United States after McTigue had figured in some exhibitions with the American.

He only tried rugby league after being asked to play for the Giants Hall colliery team where he worked and, after only eight games, Wigan signed him as a centre in 1950. McTigue's impact was not instant; he struggled to break into the first-team, a situation not helped by two years' national service in Ireland, and it was only in 1954 that he switched to prop and was given a real chance. He never looked back.

Polite, gentle and private away from the pitch, McTigue had freakish abilities on it, and he became the cornerstone of a dominant pack.

His ability to offload the ball – a skill he honed playing basketball – was sheer wizardry, and he won Challenge Cup honours in 1958, 1959 (for which he won the Lance Todd trophy) and 1965.

Feared by opponents, revered by teammates, McTigue made his Test debut in the famous Battle of Brisbane in 1958, when a depleted Great Britain side beat Australia 25-18. Kangaroos great John Raper later said that McTigue, who won a total of 25 caps, was one of the toughest opponents he had ever faced. McTigue died in 1982.

1951 - 1966

Brian McTigue cast an imposing figure in the forwards. Here he prepares to pack down against Leigh in 1960.

Brian McTigue nearly carved a career out in boxing
before deciding on rugby league.

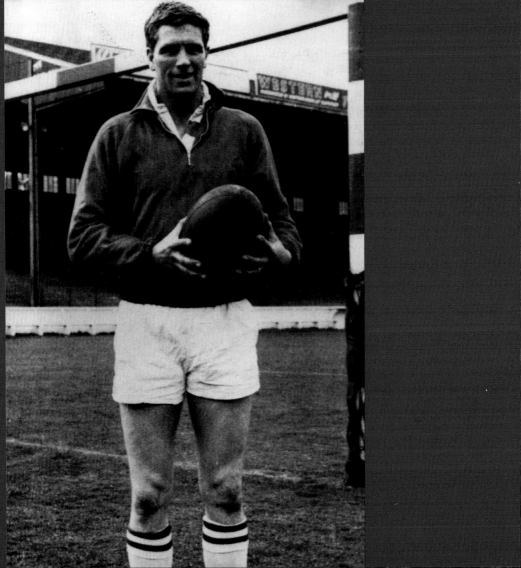

Crowds applauded as Ashton left the Central Park pitch for the last time.

Half of the greatest and most celebrated centre-wing combination in Wigan's illustrious history, Eric Ashton's name is synonymous with Billy Boston. It is hard to think of one without the other.

Ashton was a gem of a centre, famed for carving out try after try for Boston with his deceptive pace and neat inside balls.

His tally of 231 tries and 448 goals in 497 appearances points to his own scoring abilities, while Ashton's leadership abilities were obvious early in his career – he was made captain at the age of 22, and kept the role for the rest of his career.

A classy player, Ashton produced a vintage performance as an emergency stand-off when Wigan beat Wakefield to win the 1960 Championship in front of more than 80,000 fans at Bradford's Odsal Stadium. He won the Challenge Cup in 1958, 1959 and 1965.

Ashton came to Wigan's attention after word spread of his exploits playing rugby union for the Army, and he waited until his service was over before signing at Central Park. He began his 18-year association with the club by scoring two tries as a winger on his debut, but it wasn't long before he moved to the centre and Boston came onto his right flank.

Ashton played 26 internationals for Great Britain, 15 of those as captain, and became player-coach in 1963. He retired as a player in 1969 and left his role as coach four years later, moving to his hometown club St Helens the following year.

It is difficult to gauge levels of respect and affection, but the fact that Ashton was held in the highest esteem by both Wigan and St Helens fans until, and following, his death in 2008, speaks volumes of his conduct as a player, coach and person.

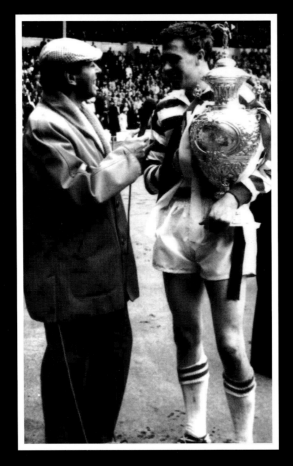

Eric Ashton is interviewed after winning the
Challenge Cup, a competition he won three times
as a player, in 1958, 1959 and 1965.

Eric Ashton scoots in for another try.

Billy BOSTON

Fans old enough to remember Billy Boston in action feel privileged that they saw him play.

Known simply as 'Billy B', he had the frame of a forward but the speed of a dashing three-quarter – a potent combination that made him arguably the most awesome winger the game has ever seen. Once he exploded, he was like a steam train. And about as easy to stop.

"Tackle him?" St Helens full-back Austen Rhodes once remarked. "Blimey... I only just managed to get out of his way!"

The sixth of 11 children, Boston grew up in Cardiff's Tiger Bay – he was childhood friends with Shirley Bassey – and alerted Wigan's scouts when he scored six tries in the Army Cup Final.

A crowd of 8,500 watched his debut for Wigan in an 'A' team match against Barrow, and after less than a dozen games of league he was selected for the 1954 tour of Australia – becoming the first black player to play for the Lions. He scored a staggering 36 tries in 18 matches Down Under, toured eight years later and played in the World Cups of 1957 and 1960. He was a points-scoring machine. He scored his first century of tries in just 68 appearances, and finished with 571 career tries in first-class matches, the most by any British player, and only surpassed by the Australian Brian Bevan. In three seasons he scored 50 or more tries, with 60 in 1956/57, and his final tally with Wigan was 478 tries in 485 games.

Boston had six visits to Wembley with Wigan between 1958 and 1966, but he cast his legacy at Central Park, where cries of "Give it Billy" could often be heard from the Kop. If he was injured, Wigan would try to suppress news of his absence because it would affect the gate.

He retired in 1968 (he played briefly for Blackpool the following year), was inducted into the Hall of Fame in 1988 and awarded an MBE in 1996.

1953 - 1968

Boston scores a try. Note the straw at the side of the pitch that
was used to cover the turf pre-match so that it wouldn't freeze.

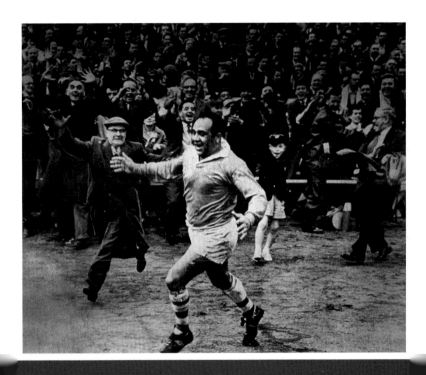

Remember this? Billy Boston crosses the line for yet another try at Central Park.

1950s

Mick SULLIVAN

Mick Sullivan is welcomed to Wigan by Billy Boston and Eric Ashton.

A fearless and ferocious winger, Mick Sullivan was the ultimate big-game player. He was once described as "the Rocky Marciano" of rugby league, and few who saw him or played with or against him would disagree.

His cold statistics make impressive reading. He set the record for Great Britain caps with 46, tries with 41, and was twice transferred for world record fees – £9,500 from Huddersfield to Wigan and £11,000 from Wigan to St Helens.

But Sullivan contributed so much more that was not recorded in the history books, but was forever imprinted in fans' memories – a punishing tackling style that defied his stature of 5ft 10ins and 13 stone.

Sullivan played on the opposite flank to Billy Boston and the big Welshman reports that while Sullivan's record in the league "wasn't anything special, in big matches he was the best".

No more was that evident than in the third Test in Sydney in 1958 when he scored a hat-trick and kept the Australians at bay with his robust tackling.

As if to underline his reputation as a showman, some of the Australian fans – frustrated with his all-action and aggressive display – threw oranges at him: legend has it that Sullivan picked up one orange, peeled it and ate it on the pitch!

1957 - 1961

Mick Sullivan won 46 caps for Great Britain.

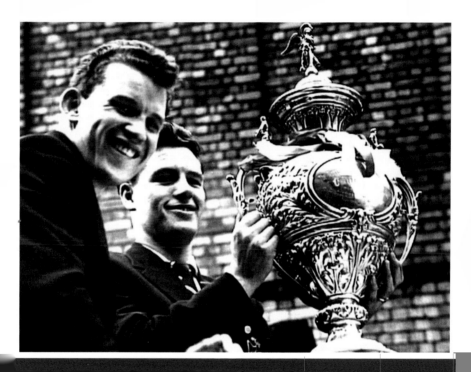

Cup, won for the second
at Hull 30-13.

1950s

Brian Nordgren's transfer to Wigan showed signs of his future career as a lawyer. When the New Zealand Rugby League claimed Wigan had breached the league's poaching signing laws, Nordgren pointed out that the international ban had expired in 1941 during the war.

He was a junior sprint champion in his native country, and the fleet-footed winger has an enviable record at Wigan, having scored more tries (312) than he made appearances (294). Not many players can boast such an impressive strike-rate.

International call-ups allowed Nordgren to make rapid progress immediately after arriving in Wigan in 1946.

He played in the Challenge Cup Final at Wembley, scoring two tries in a 13-12 defeat and won the Championship (beating Huddersfield 13-4) two weeks later.

Nordgren was also a dependable goal-kicker, booting 109 goals for Wigan. He never played for New Zealand, though he did represent 'Other Nationalities' against France in 1950. He finished that season with a staggering 57 tries for Wigan, placing him top of the try chart, and he enjoyed success in the Championship (1950 and 1952), Challenge Cup (1951) as well as the Lancashire Cup in 1949, in which he scored a competition record four tries in the final. He died in his native New Zealand in 2007.

Brian Nordgren joined Wigan from New Zealand.

Nordgren scored more tries (312) for Wigan than
he made appearances (294).

1960s

David BOLTON

David Bolton lit up Central Park with his electrifying skills.

This elusive stand-off seemed destined for greatness as soon as he scored two tries on his debut as a 17-year-old.

A graduate of the All Saints School in Wigan, he played his junior career at scrum-half but soon made the stand-off berth his own.

His electric breaks could penetrate even the best-drilled defences, and Bolton's tactical awareness and crisp distribution benefited his talented back-line players.

Bolton, who was signed by Wigan aged 15, also had a majestic boot – he was able to place towering bombs near the opposition line.

His abilities earned him representative honours, and he forged a formidable Test partnership with the brilliantly-gifted Alex Murphy, though his 1958 tour of Australia ended when he broke his collarbone in the infamous Battle of Brisbane.

A Wembley winner in 1958 and 1959, Bolton toured Down Under in 1962 and moved to Australia two years later, where he made a huge impression at Balmain.

David Bolton was a classy stand-off.

After leaving Wigan, David Bolton enjoyed great
success in Australia.

Trevor LAKE

Trevor Lake is unique for the fact that he is the only Wigan legend from the African country of Rhodesia (now Zimbabwe).

But he is fondly remembered by many for much more than a piece of geographical trivia.

Fans who saw him play have witnessed many golden Wigan moments over the years, but they have reserved a special place in their memory banks for arguably Lake's most fabulous moment: the scene was Wembley, the year was 1965, the opponents were Hunslet, and Lake's second try was a spectacular dive in the corner to evade the clutches of a desperate tackler.

Lake had trials for the South African national rugby union team before arriving at Central Park with John Winton in 1962. At first he proved to be an able deputy for the injured Billy Boston, scoring two tries on his debut at Oldham, and soon he had cemented a regular place in the Wigan side.

He finished the 1964–65 season as the league's top scorer with 40 tries, and by the time his Wigan career ended he had scored 132 tries in 140 games.

Lake's 40 tries in the 1964/65 season made him the
league's top scorer.

Trevor Lake flies in for a stunning try at Wembley against Hunslet in 1965.

1960s

Colin CLARKE

The term 'wearing his heart on his sleeve' could have been coined for Colin Clarke.

He played with ferocity and fire while serving his hometown club for a decade and a half after signing from Orrell RU as a 17-year-old.

Clarke was a real master of his craft, able to break at speed and aggravate opposition forwards with his combative approach.

The best way to illustrate how much influence Colin Clarke had on the Wigan side is to look at how they fared when he didn't play.

At Wembley in 1966, in an era when the scrum role of a hooker was a real art, Clarke was suspended for the match. St Helens mercilessly exploited his absence by giving away off-side penalties when Wigan had the ball. The rule at the time was that the non-offending team had a kick to touch, and contemporary match reports state that experienced Saints No.9, Bill Sayer, won the scrums 16-8 (not quite as comprehensively as legend has it). The loophole was later closed, but Saints still lifted the trophy.

The previous year, Clarke had played an instrumental role in an epic Challenge Cup Final against Hunslet and he also won the Lancashire Cup three times.

A 12-game spell at Salford and three matches at Leigh at the end of his career were followed by a return to Wigan, where as co-coach he guided the club to Challenge Cup Final glory in 1985 – two decades after their last Wembley triumph, when Clarke was playing.

1963 - 1978

Colin Clarke crosses for a try early in his career.

Wigan players Peter Rowe and Colin Clarke shave in the dressing room, February 1968.

Alan Davies was a winger's dream.

The centre had already made his name in a great Oldham side before being lured to Central Park in 1961, and he fitted seamlessly into a team peppered with great players.

Davies was tough and uncompromising, a lethal defender who would thwart overlaps by rushing the opposition stand-off.

His talents were not restricted to defence; he had pace and skill, and both Trevor Lake and Frank Carlton excelled from his unselfish distribution after drawing in opposing defenders.

Leigh-born Davies could also score tries himself, crossing the line a total of 52 times in 132 appearances for Wigan.

He had played 20 times for Great Britain when Wigan signed him from Oldham, but did not play for his country again, and was the only Wigan three-quarter not selected for the 1962 Lions tour.

1960s

He missed his first Wembley final through illness and saw his career cut short by injury, but in between, Roy Evans earned plenty of honours and praise in a Wigan shirt.

A local lad, he was signed from Spring View for £200 in 1957 and made his debut later that year against Swinton.

Fit, strong in the tackle and a no-nonsense performer, Evans ran good angles and punched holes in defences. He was deceptively quick, too, and switched to the loose forward position soon after breaking into the Wigan side.

He received a winners' medal despite missing Wigan's Challenge Cup Final in 1958 because he was sick, and took home another the following year.

In 1959 there was no question that he earned it, playing a key role in the team that hammered Hull by 30-13. Evans also won a Championship (1960) and two Lancashire League titles (1958/59 and 1961/62) before being called into the Great Britain squad for their tour of Australia in 1962.

Evans was forced to hang up his boots while still in his prime at the age of 27 because of a persistent groin problem. He died in 1987.

Taking on St Helens' Vince Karalius, with Brian McTigue looking on.

Wigan paid Featherstone Rovers a junior-record £1,500 for 16-year-old William Lloyd Francis; he soon repaid their investment.

He made his debut, five days after signing, against the now-defunct Liverpool City in March 1964 and served Wigan for more than a decade in the three-quarters.

Fast and alert on the left wing, Francis was equally at home in the centre berth and was popular for his strong tackling style.

He was Wigan's top try-scorer with 29 in 1967/68 and the following year was the No.1 try-scorer in rugby league, with 40. But Francis was more than a points-scorer, and after leaving Central Park for St Helens he established himself at stand-off.

Francis suffered Challenge Cup and Championship defeats with Wigan in 1970 and 1971, though he did enjoy success in the Lancashire Cup in 1971 and again two years later.

He also graced the international stage though, oddly, after playing for Great Britain against Australia in 1967, he had to wait a full decade for his next call to the Test team. Though born in Featherstone, he also represented Wales through the ancestry ruling.

Francis scored more tries than any other player
in the league in the 1968/69 season.

The Wigan dressing room at Central Park around 1975 with, from left to right, Bob
Blackwood, Colin Clarke, Green Vigo, John Martindale (kit man), Keith Mills (physio), Jimmy
Nulty, Tony Korelias, Brian Gregory, Bernard Coyle, Bill Francis and George Fairbairn

Doug LAUGHTON

Doug Laughton really was a class act.

A no-nonsense, robust player and natural leader, his arrival acted as a catalyst for a surge in fortunes for the club.

Laughton captained Wigan at Wembley in 1970 when they lost to Castleford and in the Championship, which they lost to St Helens. He enjoyed trophy success in the Lancashire Cup (1971), Floodlit Trophy (1968), Lancashire League (1969/70) and League Leaders Trophy (1970/71).

Wigan paid £6,000 to St Helens for Laughton and sold him for the same fee to Widnes six years later.

During that time, they received outstanding service from the tough, ball-handling loose-forward.

Laughton also proved his abilities on the Test stage for Great Britain, touring in 1970 as a Wigan player.

Laughton won the Man of Steel title in 1979 and enjoyed a fabulous coaching career with his hometown club Widnes and later Leeds, luring Jonathan Davies, Alan Tait and Martin Offiah from union to league. He never lost his sense of humour – when asked about one rugby union trialist, he once quipped: "That lad's got deceptive pace. He's even slower than he looks."

1967 - 1973

Laughton was a tough loose forward.

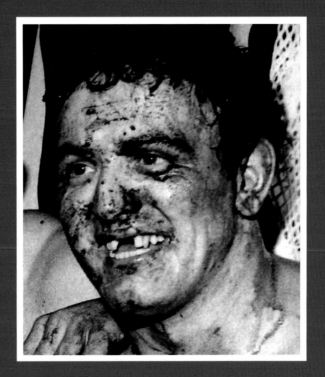
Doug Laughton shows off his smile.

1970s

Bill ASHURST

Bill Ashurst was a hard man, but blessed with the skills of a half-back.

Bill Ashurst was an outstanding player for Wigan during the 1970s.

The centre turned second row forward was a hard man of the game during a brutal era.

But such grit was forged with grace, and Ashurst was as constructive as he was destructive. By his own admission, he was not the greatest trainer and he never needed to be; his hulking body was magnificently equipped with ball-handling and kicking skills that any half-back would envy.

A real showman, the former Rose Bridge amateur became a hugely popular figure at his hometown club, helping Wigan reach Challenge Cup and Championship finals in 1970 and 1971 respectively. The club lost both, but Ashurst won the prestigious Harry Sunderland trophy for his performance in the latter, while legend has it that the announcer misread the Lance Todd Trophy winner as 'Bill Kirkbride' (instead of 'Bill Ashurst') in the 1970 Wembley final.

If success in Australia can act as a measure of greatness, then Ashurst can be regarded as one of the best.

Twice a record signing in his career, he was a phenomenon at Penrith Panthers, so much so that there were stories of him selling Man of the Match prizes before he had even played in games. He was later named as Penrith's greatest-ever second row forward. After returning to Wigan as coach he became a born-again Christian, but that was not the end of his colourful playing career. He briefly came out of retirement aged 40 for one match for Runcorn and was sent off for head-butting Wigan's Andy Goodway.

1968 - 1973, 1977 - 1978

A local lad, Bill Ashurst was a second row forward and a skilled goal kicker. In all he made 179 appearances between and 1968 and 1977, scored 74 tries and 146 goals. He never toured but won three Great Britain caps.

Wigan Rugby League great, Bill Ashurst, with his son, Billy junior, in 1987.

Dave ROBINSON

In the annals of world record rugby league signings, Dave Robinson's name can often be overlooked.

But after Wigan broke the bank to land him from Swinton in 1969 for £10,000, he gave the club sterling service for five years.

The blond-haired Lancashire lad was a classy loose forward whose big commodity was a precious quality – consistency.

A gent off the pitch, Robinson was already a Great Britain international by the time he arrived at Central Park and he went on to make 145 appearances in the cherry and white shirt, scoring 17 tries.

He was skilful with the ball and though he wasn't the biggest of forwards, he was raw-boned, and a highly effective tackler.

Very fit and mobile, Robinson's arrival galvanised a formidable pack that included the likes of Bill Ashurst, Doug Laughton and Colin Clarke.

In the season he signed, Wigan won the Lancashire League and legend has it that even though Robinson had only played 12 games – three short of the 15 matches required to receive a medal – he was presented with a medal as the league organisers didn't want the controversy of the game's record signing going home empty handed!

1969 - 1974

Robinson, second from left, playing for Great Britain.

Dave Robinson crosses for a try.

It bordered on the ridiculous just how good George Fairbairn was in a terrible team.

To say he was a shining light would be a harsh understatement – he carried the side heroically during a turbulent period, and many agree that the only reason Wigan were worth watching in the late '70s was because of Fairbairn's sparkling performances.

To put his impact into perspective, at the lowest point in Wigan's history the club were relegated at the end of the 1979/80 season, yet Fairbairn still won the prized Man of Steel award that year. He was also Wigan's only Great Britain tourist.

An elegant runner who lit up Central Park with his lively attacks, Fairbairn was a talented goal-kicker and a courageous defender.

Although from Peebles, in Scotland, and a former Kelso rugby union player, Fairbairn represented both Lancashire (twice) and England (15 caps, including the 1975 World Cup) during his stellar career and went on to captain Great Britain.

Fairbairn became player-coach and guided Wigan to promotion in 1980/81, but was replaced as coach by Maurice Bamford and never played for the club again.

He became such a fans' favourite that when Wigan sold him to Hull KR for a then-record £72,500, there were demonstrations against the club's decision.

The way they were in the '70s: Wigan full-back George Fairbairn takes on Saints' Billy Benyon and Harry Pinner at Knowsley Road in a Premiership first round tie in 1977

signing.

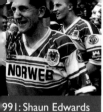

1991: Shaun Edwards collecting his medal, by Denis Betts, after t Helens in 1991.

A former dual-code schoolboys captain, he was always de for greatness from the moment he signed with Wigan at on his 17th birthday.

The most decorated rugby league player ever and a Chall Cup finalist 11 times (nine as a winner, including captaining side in 1988 aged just 21), there are examples throughout glittering career that illustrate his importance and ample c

Toughness? See the 1990 Challenge Cup Final, when he fi the match despite a broken eye socket – a heroic act that

the Man of Steel award later that year.

though he started his career at full-back and ended it at scrum-half, Edwards is d for playing stand-off outside Andy Gregory, a lethal combination that was fea the game.

knack of supporting play earned him many of his 274 tries from his 467 appear bench) for his hometown club, including 43 tries in the 1992/93 season and a c lling ten in one match, at Swinton in 1992.

dwards became a master of his art by analysing the game with scientific scrutin surprising that, since retiring as a player, he has made such a huge impact coach

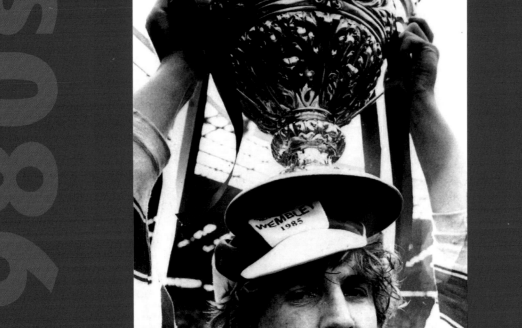

Brett KENNY

Sports writer Paul Wilson once described Brett Kenny as "the sort of stand-off you would be in your dreams".

It's hard to disagree. Graced with fabulous speed and swerve, he didn't so much run through defences as glide through them.

The title of his autobiography – *The Natural* – hints at his freakish, uncoachable abilities. The Kangaroos Test stand-off only played at Wigan for one campaign during an off-season with his Australian club Parramatta, but fans still eulogise about his obscene amount of talent, and Kenny is widely regarded as the club's greatest ever Australian recruit.

His statistics of 19 tries in 25 appearances are impressive. But it was his dashing, Lance Todd Trophy-winning display in the 1985 Challenge Cup Final victory over Hull that is etched in most memories, not least as it helped bring the famous silverware back to Wigan for the first time in two decades.

Little wonder many still refer to that epic match as 'The Brett Kenny Final'.

Brett Kenny strides over for a try against Hull at Wembley in 1985.

Brett Kenny and John Ferguson show off the Challenge Cup.

1980s

Dean Bell was known as 'Mean Dean' for his fearless approach.

The words rhyme, but that was not the only reason he was known as 'Mean Dean'.

At a time when Wigan embraced a full-time era, Dean Bell was the consummate professional.

Tough, uncompromising and a natural leader, the former Central Park and New Zealand Test captain was Graham Lowe's first signing as coach and he remains one of Wigan's greatest ever overseas recruits.

His unforgiving approach was best illustrated in his ferocious tackling technique, and his strengths were not limited to defending.

Fast enough to play on the wing and strong enough to fill in at loose forward, Bell was hugely popular for his full-on approach and will to win.

Bell was a Wembley winner seven times (he won the Lance Todd Trophy in 1993, as captain), and it's easier to list the trophies he didn't win than did (he was injured for Wigan's World Club Challenge triumphs in 1987 and 1991).

The Man of Steel in 1992, he came back to Wigan in 2000 to oversee youth development before returning to his homeland to take up a similar role with the New Zealand Warriors in 2007.

Dean Bell with Wigan's Australian coach John Monie.

Wigan coach Graham Lo   enderson Gill ready for

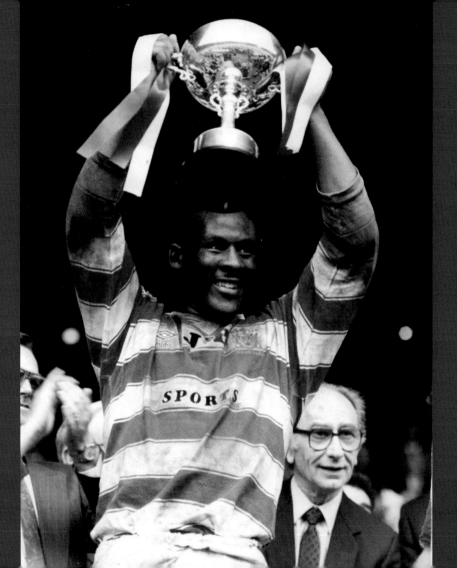

1980s

Ellery HANLEY

The most incredible player of his era and, some will say, any era.

Hanley's influence in the all-conquering Wigan side of the late '80s and early '90s cannot be overstated.

This swashbuckling, powerful and pacy loose forward was in a different class to most of the players he faced.

He announced himself to the wider rugby league community with a stunning length-of-the-field try for Bradford and – after a world-record transfer to Wigan – he cast a glorious legacy at the club, scoring 189 tries in 202 appearances, a magnificent strike-rate for a forward.

An immense athlete, his former teammates still wax lyrical about Hanley's singular focus and extraordinary fitness; and his freakish ability to produce match-winning performances proved inspirational. A dangerous runner with an explosive fend, Hanley was twice winner of the Man of Steel and became the first Briton to win the Golden Boot as the world's best player.

Hanley also had the rare distinction of being a huge success Down Under with Balmain, Western Suburbs and the British Lions. The Australians respected him so much that they christened him 'The Black Pearl'. Hanley captained Wigan in three Wembley triumphs (1989, 1990 and 1991) before moving to Leeds for £250,000. He was later inducted into rugby league's Hall of Fame.

1985 - 1991

Wembley, 1988: Ellery Hanley evades the cover to score against Halifax.

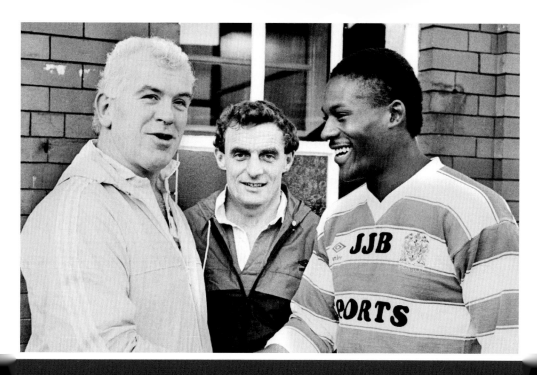

Wigan Rugby League legend Ellery Hanley is welcomed by joint coaches Colin Clarke and Alan McInnes after signing in 1985.

Andy GREGORY

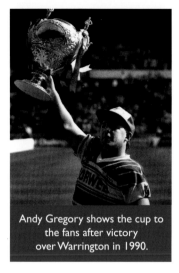

Andy Gregory shows the cup to the fans after victory over Warrington in 1990.

Always cunning, often colourful and occasionally controversial, Andy Gregory was the finest half-back of his generation.

Inimitable and unmissable with his sleeves rolled up and confident swagger, he was a real pocket battleship of a scrum-half whose partnership with Shaun Edwards seemed to border on the telepathic at times. Gregory was born and bred in Wigan but earned his fame at Widnes, helping them beat his hometown club in the 1984 Challenge Cup Final, before he was lured to Central Park after a stint at Warrington.

Gregory was a firecracker, able to command his star-studded backline, control the intensity of a game and also take on and beat defenders himself.

His success on three Lions tours and for Illawarra made him popular in Australia, with some labelling him a 'milk bottle' because of his pale complexion. Gregory crafted arguably the most famous Great Britain try ever, evading a clutch of Kangaroos defenders to unleash his namesake, Mike Gregory, to the line in a famous 26-12 win in Sydney. Gregory twice won the Lance Todd Trophy as Man of the Match in a Challenge Cup Final.

His record for Wigan included two World Club Challenge triumphs (1987 and 1991) and five Wembley victories (he also had two while playing for Widnes). Gregory later played for Salford and, as coach of the Reds, ended Wigan's unbeaten eight-year Challenge Cup run in 1996.

1987 - 1992

Andy Gregory is besieged by autograph hunters after a match against Workington in January 1987

Shaun Edwards passes for Andy Gregory to score against Saints at Wembley in 1989, with Gary Connolly floored.

Frano BOTICA

Three things seemed certain in the 1990s – death, taxes, and Frano Botica's successful conversion attempts.

No matter where he was in the opposition's half, the New Zealander had an uncanny, undisputed and unrivalled ability to strike goals.

Incredibly, for a player with such deadly accuracy with the boot, Botica wasn't signed as a points-scoring machine.

A former All Blacks international, he initially struggled to make his mark after his £200,000 switch, and mastered the art of goal-kicking as a way to secure his place in a side that had a galaxy of stars.

His talents were not restricted to kicking however, and after moving from wing to stand-off following Andy Gregory's departure, he became a huge hit among the Central Park faithful, with one of his finest displays being in Wigan's World Club Challenge 21-4 triumph over Penrith in which he also won the Man of the Match award.

In total, he kicked 827 goals in 179 appearances, but those impressive statistics don't go near to doing justice to Botica's legacy as a goal-scoring sensation.

His marksmanship with the boot allowed him to continue playing in union well past an age when most retired, before returning to his homeland.

1990 - 1995

Frano Botica won the Man of the Match award in the World Club Challenge victory over Penrith.

Frano Botica celebrates Wigan's Challenge Cup success in
1994 with fellow Kiwis Sam Panapa and Inga Tuigamala.

Gary CONNOLLY

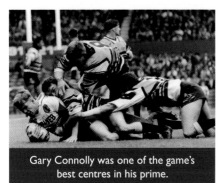
Gary Connolly was one of the game's best centres in his prime.

Not all teen prodigies fulfil their potential, but Gary Connolly certainly did.

Enviably talented and an elegant runner, he started and finished his career at full-back but made a name for himself at Wigan as a centre. And what a centre he was.

Unselfish with the ball, Connolly had freakish upper body strength (his arm wrestling abilities are legendary in league circles) and his one-on-one tackling severely rationed oppositions' scoring chances.

He was a sensation when he burst onto the scene at hometown club St Helens as a 17-year-old and had already toured with Great Britain when Wigan signed him for £250,000 in 1993.

It is a measure of Connolly's incredible success at Wigan that St Helens fans still call him 'Judas' more than a decade after his defection.

The then-England Rugby Union captain Will Carling described Connolly as "the best centre in world rugby" during his first, brief flirt with union in 1996/97. Carling is also credited for giving him his nickname 'Lager'.

Connolly, who enjoyed a successful stint with Australian club Canterbury, played 31 times for Great Britain and four times for England.

He was one of only two Britons included in the Rest of the World side in 1997 – along with Jason Robinson – and the following year won the inaugural Grand Final. Initially leaving Wigan in 2002 for Leeds via Orrell, where he won the Lance Todd Trophy, he returned in 2004 before ending his career with stints at Widnes and Munster RUFC.

1993 - 2004

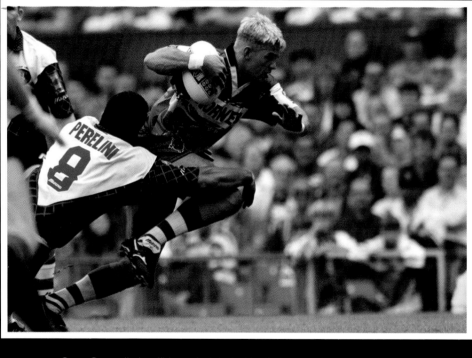

Gary Connolly is still branded 'Judas' by St Helens fans - a mark of his success with their arch-rivals Wigan.

Gary Connolly touches down to score for Wigan against his former club, St Helens, during the Challenge Cup Final at Murrayfield, Edinburgh, in 2002.

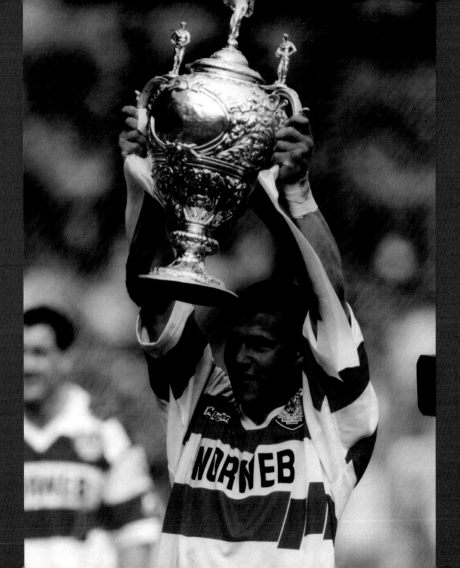

Jason Robinson says his farewell to Central Park after a final game against St Helens.

There were few better sights in rugby league than watching Jason Robinson get the ball... and go.

Energetic, explosive and evasive, Robinson was one of Wigan's most exciting attacking players.

He was signed from Hunslet Parkside amateur club as a half-back but, on the persuasion of his mentor John Monie, switched to the wing.

It was an inspired move, which in turn inspired hundreds of glorious memories.

His dazzling acceleration and under-rated toughness paved the way for a sparkling career with Wigan that included success in the World Club Challenge (1994), Challenge Cup (1993, 1995), Championship (1992, 1993, 1994, 1995 and 1996) and Super League (1998).

He scored 171 tries in 281 appearances and was a catalyst for many more tries because his electric bursts would often spread panic through opposition defences. Nicknamed Billy Whizz after the *Beano* comic character, Robinson's personal life was hugely influenced by Va'aiga Tuigamala and, under his guidance, he became a born-again Christian.

As he matured he never lost his boyish appetite, finishing as Wigan's leading try-scorer in five consecutive years until his departure in 2000. Robinson became a trailblazer for league players switching to union – though none enjoyed his level of success – with Sale Sharks and the British Lions. He scored England's only try in their World Cup triumph in 2003 and retired – with an MBE – in 2007 as a legend of both codes.

Wembley, 1995: Jason Robinson is congratulated
for a try by Henry Paul. Robinson won the Lance
Todd Trophy for his efforts.

Va'aiga Tuigamala sends Jason Robinson off down the wing.

1990s

Martin OFFIAH

Martin Offiah's two biggest traits as a Wigan player are best illustrated by a Nike advert in which he starred next to the slogan, "Your hands can't catch what your eyes can't see." Firstly, that he was fast and, secondly, that he was famous.

Lavishly gifted with speed, there was no catching Offiah and his searing pace helped him become the third all-time top try-scorer in the game with 501 from 477 matches.

He played briefly in rugby union at the beginning and end of his career, but it was league that would make him a superstar, and even today he remains one of the sport's few nationally-recognised names.

After transferring from Widnes to Wigan for a then-world record £440,000, Offiah added a lethal edge to a backline already bristling with talent.

He patrolled the left touchline with predatory instincts and was also alert to midfield breaks... and quick enough to finish them off.

The jet-heeled winger had his critics for his questionable defence, but most fans loved him, and even mis-pronounced his surname so they could bestow him with the nickname 'Chariots' (his name should be pronounced 'Off-e-ah' rather than 'O-fire').

He scored 26 tries in 33 games for Great Britain and enjoyed three stints in Australia, while his length-of-the-field try in the 1994 Challenge Cup Final against Leeds is one of the greatest ever seen at Wembley Stadium.

Awarded an MBE for services to the game, his spells at London Broncos, Salford and Wasps RUFC were followed by a move into TV work and acting.

1992 - 1996

Martin Offiah is mobbed by fans during the 1992 Challenge Cup
homecoming celebrations.

Offiah's length-of-the-field try at Wembley in 1995 against Leeds.

Denis BETTS

Denis Betts soaks up a Challenge Cup homecoming.

Only two men have ever captained England in a World Cup Final at Wembley Stadium. The first was Bobby Moore in 1966. The second was Denis Betts in 1995.

Betts' career, though, is far more than a piece of pub quiz trivia, and though he didn't manage to emulate Moore's achievement of winning a World Cup at Wembley, his long and distinguished career had far more triumphs than failures.

The Salfordian grew up just miles from Old Trafford and even had trials with Manchester United as a youngster before embarking on a rugby league career. Signed from Leigh Rangers amateurs, he made his full debut on the wing but soon became a key member of the all-conquering Wigan side. Betts' pace down the flank was often destructive and he became the model of the modern second row forward, being both a workhorse and a thoroughbred.

At the age of just 21 he won the Lance Todd Trophy at Wembley and went on to make 32 appearances for Great Britain. His polished performances earned him the coveted Man of Steel in 1995 before his long career with Wigan was interrupted by a three-year spell at the Auckland Warriors.

After hanging up his boots, he joined the coaching staff at the JJB Stadium but was thrust into the top job when Mike Gregory was taken ill, and later left to join Gloucester Rugby Union Club's coaching staff.

1986 - 1995, 1998 - 2001

Denis Betts celebrates after scoring Wigan's first ever try at the JJB Stadium in 1999, during a play-off defeat against Castleford.

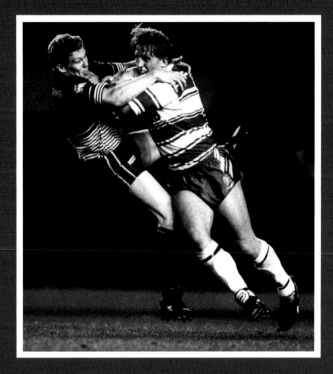

Denis Betts takes on Penrith in the 1991 World
Club Challenge.

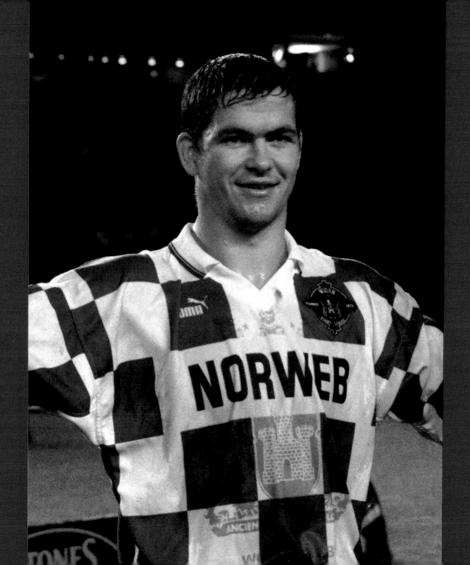

A colossus of a man, in terms of both stature and physique, Andy Farrell was the complete package.

Once described as being a half-back trapped in a forward's body, he burst onto the Wigan scene as a 16-year-old try-scoring substitute in 1991 and became the cornerstone of the Wigan side for more than a decade.

An inspirational leader, he was able to break defences with a rampaging charge, a measured kick or a bullet-like pass that could cut out several defenders.

It seemed there was nothing he couldn't do, a claim he strengthened when he took over the goal-kicking duties following Frano Botica's departure in 1995.

A staggering 1,355 goals later, he is second only to the mighty Jim Sullivan in the club's all-time goal-scoring and point-scoring records.

Farrell led Wigan to the inaugural Grand Final in 1998 and Challenge Cup in 2002, was twice named Man of Steel (1996 and 2004) and became only the second Briton after Ellery Hanley to win the Golden Boot as the world's best player (also in 2004).

Though he never enjoyed a series win at international level, his record was enviable: he became Great Britain's youngest Test forward aged 18, was captain by 21 and he made an amazing sequence of 34 consecutive appearances for his country from 1993 to 2004. He was awarded an OBE in the 2005 New Year Honours list before switching codes to rugby union with Saracens and England.

Captain Courageous: Andy Farrell played on despite horrendous injuries to his nose

Farrell kicked a staggering 1,355 goals for Wigan.

Kris RADLINSKI

There was never a shred of doubt over Kris Radlinski's stature as a Wigan great. But had there been, that would have been swept away when he came out of retirement to play for the team for free during Wigan's flirt with relegation in 2006.

Radlinski was one of the world's most complete and respected full-backs, and was the sort of clubman who made you proud to be a Wigan fan.

A whole-hearted player who sought perfection from his own performances, he cut down opponents with bone-jarring tackles and was so safe at the back that he would foil even the greatest exponents of the high kick.

Radlinski edged into his hometown club's first-team in October 1993 and instantly sparkled; within two years he had cemented his place in a slick backline containing the likes of Jason Robinson, Martin Offiah, Gary Connolly and Va'aiga Tuigamala.

Aged 19, he became the first player to score a hat-trick in a Premiership Final in 1995, winning the Harry Sunderland Trophy for his efforts, and later that season replicated his sterling form at full-back for England in the World Cup.

Radlinski was an impeccable support player and once he turned on his afterburners, he was virtually unstoppable; a virtue that earned him 183 tries in his Wigan career, including 30 in one season in 2001.

Such a prolific strike-rate alerted the RFU, but Radlinski rejected their lucrative overtures on two occasions to stay loyal to his hometown club.

He climbed off his sick bed with a badly infected foot to win the Lance Todd Trophy for his try-saving exploits against St Helens in the 2002 Challenge Cup Final, and the following year, the 20-Test veteran captained Great Britain against New Zealand. After retiring for a second (and final) time, he was awarded an MBE for his services to rugby league.

1993 - 2006

Kris Radlinski races club great Shaun Edwards, who was playing for London, in 1997.

Kris Radlinski's finest hour, lifting the Challenge Cup in 2002 after climbing off his sickbed to play.

Brett DALLAS

Challenge Cup Final, St Helens v Wigan: Brett Dallas and Terry O'Connor.

With a name to rival any Hollywood hero, Brett Dallas was once described as being "so fast he could catch and kiss a bullet".

The speed-merchant arrived at Wigan in 2000 at the relatively young age of 25 after a sterling career Down Under, in which he was the youngest player to represent Queensland (aged 18, in 1993) and had won a World Cup with Australia in 1995.

Dallas scored an impressive 21 tries in 24 games in his first season, his blistering pace making him one of the quickest in the competition – though speed was certainly not his only quality. The role of the modern winger has changed, and Dallas certainly got the scars to prove it.

He drove the ball in with a reckless enthusiasm, despite frequently being tackled high, and he was as tough as he was consistent – traits that are hard to find even in the very best wingers.

A model professional who commanded respect, Dallas' injury problems owed as much to his fearless style as they did to bad luck, but during difficult seasons in 2005 and 2006 his performances shone like a beacon. "He never played badly. Never," commented fellow great, Dean Bell.

Dallas twice resisted offers to return to Australia, and ended his seven-year association in 2006 when, in the final match of the season, he signalled his departure by leaving his boots in the centre of the pitch, an act that prompted a rousing and emotional applause.

2000 - 2006

Dallas leaves behind his boots in an emotional farewell to Wigan in 2006.

Adrian LAM

Adrian Lam is head over heels at landing a try in Wigan's 70-12 demolition of Swinton.

An American sports commentator once remarked how crazy the world seemed "when the best rapper out there is white and the best golfer is black".

In 2002, you could add to that list '...and the best Super League player is a 30-something Papua New Guinean'.

Adrian Lam won the coveted Players' Player of the Year award that season after a sparkling campaign. A veteran of the NRL with the Sydney Roosters and a former Queensland captain, Lam is the only player ever to take part in State of Origin games and to captain a country other than Australia.

The scrum-half was a revelation at Wigan in a position that had become something of a poisoned chalice since Shaun Edwards' exit in 1997.

His small stature masked a steely resolve and toughness, and his love and enthusiasm for the game was obvious. He had all the skills of a classy No.7, and could unlock even the tightest of defences with a jink, step, short kick or one of an array of majestic passes. He scored 44 tries in 116 appearances, but it was as an organiser that he truly excelled.

Lam was a master-tactician, calling plays and backline moves with the authority of a military general, and it was his ability to bring out the best in his teammates that made him such an influential player.

It was little surprise that such talents made coaching a natural progression for Lam when he retired as a player, taking charge of the junior squad at Wigan before returning to Australia to take roles at Cronulla and Sydney Roosters.

Adrian Lam won the prestigious Players' Player of the Year award in 2002.

Modern Masters

Trent BARRETT

Trent Barrett was named Players' Player of the Year after a sterling first season in Super League.

When Trent Barrett arrived at Wigan, fans were soon marvelling at skills they hadn't seen in years.

Former coach Colin Clarke hailed him as the club's greatest Australian signing since Brett Kenny more than two decades earlier. Few disagreed.

Against a backdrop of recent turmoil, recent record defeats and an escape from the jaws of relegation, Barrett's immense performances dug the team out of many holes throughout the season.

Blessed with a complete range of skills, he has the rare ability to control a team, and a game, like a master puppeteer.

He scored 18 tries in his first season and was the architect for many more, leading the Warriors on a fairytale end-of-season run into and through the play-offs that ended just one match short of the Grand Final.

A veteran of 11 Tests and three tours with Australia, he conjured a remarkable comeback at Bradford with a vintage display that helped turn a 30-6 defeat into a 31-30 victory, arguably the greatest comeback in Super League history.

A former St George-Illawarra captain, and NRL Player of the Year in 2000, he finished his debut season with nearly every individual award going: Wigan Player of the Year, Players' Player of the Year, Writers' Player of the Year and the No.1 stand-off ranked in the World XIII. Even fans who had been used to being left open-jawed by Barrett couldn't believe it when he missed out on the Man of Steel prize.

2007 - PRESENT

Trent Barrett celebrates a try with Chris Ashton as Phil
Bailey comes to join in.

Subscribers

Graham Bent
David Bithell
Keith Brockley
Christine & David Cain
Peter & Lynne Carroll
Frank Clayton
Ged Cunliffe
John Cunliffe
Brian Darbyshire
Drew & Paul Darbyshire
Ron & Ann Davies, and in memory of James Valentine
Anne Demsey
John Demsey
Tracey & Anthony Derby
Roy Dickinson
Michael English
Alan Fairhurst
In memory of Mark David Fairhurst
Walter Faulkner
John David Foster
William Foster
Raymond Gee, Carl Gee, Clayton Gee
George Harris
John Higham
Malcolm Hitchen
Michael Holland
Neil Hopper
Robert Johnson
Philip James Knowles

Tommy Lawton
Vicki Lloyd
Karen Lyon
Gordon Massey
Bill McConville
Terry Middlehurst
Keith Moorfield
Arnold Moss
Terry Parkinson
Richard Parry
Philip E. Pendlebury
Deborah J. Daniels & Joseph S. Pledger
Alan Preston
Kenny Priestley
Garth L. Rigby
Karl Rutter
Ken Rutter
Brian Selwood
Mark Sherrington
J. Barry Taylor
Norman & Josephine Theaker
Mick Turner
Frank Unsworth
William Walls
Gavan Westwood
Keith Williams
Brian Winnard
Geoff Winnard
Stephen John Yates

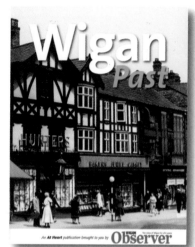

Wigan Past
£12.99
ISBN 978-1-84547-184-2

Take a step back in time, courtesy of the photographic archives of the *Wigan Observer*. This magnificent collection of pictures, taken over many years by our photographers, unearths hidden secrets from times past.

These pages reveal many facets of Wigan's rich heritage – its wonderful people, magnificent buildings, celebrity visitors and famous sporting tradition.

Many faces, young and old, beam from the pages enjoying their small moment of fame in front of the camera. The people of Wigan make the town what it is today, and the wide variety of their experiences is reflected in this book.

Take time to browse through these pages and enjoy seeing for yourself just what makes Wigan the wonderful place it is now – and always has been.

For more information: If you would like any further information on the above title please contact us at the address below.
At Heart Ltd: 32 Stamford Street, Altrincham, Cheshire, WA14 1EY **Tel:** 0161 924 0159 **Fax:** 0161 924 0160

At Heart Ltd Titles

For more information or to buy any of these titles visit www.atheart.co.uk or your local bookseller

Lancashire Titles

Pocket Belle Vue	978-1-84547-164-4	£6.99
Manchester At War	978-1-84547-096-8	£14.99
The Changing Face of Manchester Vol. 1 (Revised Edition)	978-1-84547-189-7	£12.99
The Changing Face of Manchester Vol. 2	978-1-84547-104-0	£14.99
The Changing Face of Manchester Vol. 3	978-1-84547-160-6	£12.99
The Changing Face of Manchester in the Seventies	978-1-84547-117-0	£12.99
Around Manchester in the 50s & 60s (Revised Edition)	978-1-84547-192-7	£12.99
Manchester City FC: 125 Years of Football	978-1-84547-185-9	£12.99
Lancashire's Four Seasons	978-1-84547-183-5	£12.99
The Ribble Valley in Pictures	978-1-84547-188-0	£12.99
Blackpool Then and Now	978-1-84547-153-8	£12.99
Legends: The great players of Blackpool FC	978-1-84547-182-8	£12.99
Chorley Past	978-1-84547-136-1	£12.99
Garstang Past	978-1-84547-137-8	£12.99
Wigan Past	978-1-84547-184-2	£12.99

Yorkshire Titles

Flooded Yorkshire 2007	978-1-84547-180-4	£14.99
The Great Flood	978-1-84547-150-7	£13.99
The Great South Yorkshire Floods	978-1-84547-178-1	£12.99
Leeds Past	978-1-84547-131-6	£12.99
Scarborough Past	978-1-84547-166-8	£12.99
Yorkshire At War	978-1-84547-109-5	£14.99
Yorkshire Past	978-1-84547-106-4	£14.99
Yorkshire Past: East Riding	978-1-84547-126-2	£12.99
Yorkshire Past: North Riding	978-1-84547-125-5	£12.99
Yorkshire Past: West Riding	978-1-84547-127-9	£12.99
Yorkshire's Picture Post Vol. 1	978-1-84547-097-5	£14.99
Yorkshire's Picture Post Vol. 2	978-1-84547-114-9	£16.99

Sheffield Titles

Bygone Transport: Sheffield on the Move	978-1-84547-100-2	£14.99
Sheffield FC - Celebrating 150 Years	978-1-84547-174-3	£12.99
A Year in the Garden	978-1-84547-105-7	£14.99
Sheffield at Play	978-1-84547-108-8	£14.99

Lincolnshire & Southern Counties Titles

Grantham in the News 1951-1975	978-1-84547-141-5	£12.99
Grantham in the News 1976-2000	978-1-84547-173-6	£12.99
Grantham in Focus	978-1-84547-142-2	£9.95
Mere Quacks	978-1-84547-167-5	£12.99
Skegness Past	978-1-84547-143-9	£14.99
Ipswich in the '50s & '60s	978-1-84547-102-6	£14.99
Ipswich - the War Years	978-1-84547-095-1	£12.99
Ipswich Speedway: A Decade in Pictures	978-1-84547-191-0	£12.99
Spalding Flower Parade: The Golden Years	978-1-84547-159-0	£12.99
Spalding in the Fifties	978-1-84547-158-3	£12.99
Northampton Looking Back Vol. 1	978-1-84547-157-6	£12.99
Northampton Looking Back Vol. 2	978-1-84547-186-6	£12.99
Walking in the Wolds with Hugh Marrows	978-1-84547-144-6	£8.95
Walking Through Lincolnshire's History	978-1-84547-187-3	£8.95
Worksop Past	978-1-84547-149-1	£12.99

Forthcoming Titles

Spalding in the Sixties
Kettering in Pictures
Burnley Legends
The Derbyshire Times Railway Album
Market Harborough in the '70s
Legends of Sheffield Wednesday FC
Legends of Sheffield United FC
Legends of Stockport County FC
Legends of Rochdale AFC
Sheffield Star Railway Album

For more information: If you would like any further information on any of the above titles please contact us at the address below.
At Heart Ltd: 32 Stamford Street, Altrincham, Cheshire, WA14 1EY **Tel:** 0161 924 0159 **Fax:** 0161 924 0160